AF515524

Mousses cheesecakes & cupcakes

TARLA DALAL
India's #1 Cookery Author

S&C
SANJAY & CO.
MUMBAI

COOKBOOKS BY TARLA DALAL

INDIAN COOKING
Tava Cooking
Rotis & Subzis
Desi Khana
The Complete Gujarati Cook Book
Mithai
Chaat
Achaar aur Parathe
The Rajasthani Cookbook
Swadisht Subzian
Punjabi Khana
Mughlai Khana
South Indian Recipes

WESTERN COOKING
The Complete Italian Cookbook
The Chocolate Cookbook
Eggless Desserts
Mocktails & Snacks
Thai Cooking
Soups & Salads
Mexican Cooking
Chinese Cooking
Easy Chinese Cooking
Sizzlers & Barbeques
Cakes & Pastries
Party Drinks
Wraps & Rolls
Mousses, Cheesecakes & Cupcakes New

TOTAL HEALTH
Low Calorie Healthy Cooking
Pregnancy Cookbook
Baby and Toddler Cookbook
Cooking with 1 Teaspoon of Oil
Home Remedies
Delicious Diabetic Recipes
Fast Foods Made Healthy
Healthy Soups & Salads
Healthy Breakfast
Calcium Rich Recipes
Healthy Heart Cook Book
Forever Young Diet
Healthy Snacks
Iron Rich Recipes
Healthy Juices
Low Cholesterol Recipes
Good Food for Diabetes
Healthy Subzis
Healthy Snacks for Kids
High Blood Pressure Cook Book
Low Calorie Sweets
Nutritious Recipes for Pregnancy
Diabetic Snacks
Zero Oil Rotis & Subzis
Zero Oil Soups, Salads & Snacks
Zero Oil Dal & Chawal
Acidity Cook Book
Growing Kids Cookbook
Soya Rotis & Subzis
Cooking with Sprouts
Exotic Diabetic Cooking - Part 1
Healthy Diabetic Cooking
Protein Rich Recipes
Eat Well Stay Well
Weight Loss after Pregnancy
100 Calorie Snacks
Top 10 Healthy Foods New
Healthy Starters New

MINI SERIES
Cooking Under 10 minutes
Pizzas and Pasta
Fun Food for Children
Roz ka Khana
Idlis & Dosas
Microwave Desi Khana
Paneer
Parathas
Chawal
Dals
Sandwiches
Quick Cooking
Curries & Kadhis
Chinese Recipes
Jain Desi Khana
7 Dinner Menus
Jain International Recipes
Punjabi Subzis
Chips & Dips
Corn
Microwave Subzis
Baked Dishes
Stir-Fry
Potatoes
Recipes Using Leftovers
Noodles
Lebenese
Cook Book for Two's
Know your Dals & Pulses
Fruit & Vegetable Carving
Know your Spices
Know your Flours
Popular Restaurant Gravies
Know Your Green Leafy Vegetables
Paneer Snacks
Pressure Cooker Recipes
Faraal Foods for Fasting Days
Finger Foods for Kids
Microwave Desi Khana - Part II New

GENERAL COOKING
Exciting Vegetarian Cooking
Microwave Recipes
Saatvik Khana
The Pleasures of Vegetarian Cooking
The Delights of Vegetarian Cooking
The Joys of Vegetarian Cooking
Cooking with Kids
Snacks Under 10 Minutes
Ice-Cream & Frozen Desserts
Desserts Under 10 Minutes
Entertaining
Microwave Snacks & Desserts
Kebabs & Tikkis
Non-fried Snacks
Mumbai's Roadside Snacks
Tiffin Treats for Kids New

First Printing : 2012

Copyright © Sanjay & Co.

ISBN : 978-93-80392-15-8

Price Rs. 299/-

Published & Distributed by :
SANJAY & COMPANY
353/A-1, Shah & Nahar Industrial Estate, Dhanraj Mill Compound, Lower Parel (W), Mumbai - 400 013. INDIA.
Tel. : (91-22) 4345 2400 • Fax : (91-22) 2496 5876

"Tarla Dalal" is also a registered trademark owned by Sanjay & Co.

ALL RIGHTS RESERVED WITH THE PUBLISHERS.

No portion of this book shall be reproduced, stored in retrieval system or transmitted by any means, electronic, mechanical, photocopying, recording or otherwise, without the written permission of the publishers.

Disclaimer : While every precaution has been taken in the preparation of this book, the publishers and the author assume no responsibility for errors or omissions. Neither is any liability assumed for damages resulting from the use of information contained herein.

Bulk Purchases : Tarla Dalal Cookbooks are ideal gifts. If you are interested in buying more than 500 assorted copies of Tarla Dalal Cookbooks at special prices, please contact us at 91-22-4345 2400 or email : sanjay@tarladalal.com

For books, Membership on **tarladalal.com**, Subscription for **Cooking & More** and Recipe queries
Timing : 9.30 a.m. to 6.00 p.m., Monday to Friday, 9.30 a.m. to 1.00 p.m. Saturday
Contact : Tel. : (91-22) 4345 2400 • Fax : (91-22) 2496 5876
E-mail : ravindra@tarladalal.com • sanjay@tarladalal.com

Recipe Research & Development
Nisha Katira
Payal Shah
Neha Mirlekar
Mruga Dholakia

Food Stylist
Nisha Katira

Assistant Food Stylist
Jay Bhatt

Photography
Sanjay Dalal

Copy Editor
Janani Gopalkrishnan Vikram

Design
Satyamangal Rege

Typesetting
Adityas Enterprises

Printed by
Minal Sales Agencies, Mumbai

Introduction

A perfect dessert goes well with everything else, makes you reminiscent of the earlier courses, and ties the whole meal together. Rich and creamy, they are the perfect end to any meal or party. In fact, I know some people who would even miss a course of the main meal to save space for an extra dose of the dessert. What is more, nowadays hosts are getting very creative with the desserts. Although cakes and pastries are everyone's favourite, people are thinking beyond the usual options, and exploring a larger variety including mousses, cheesecakes and cupcakes. So, to keep up with the current trends, I bring to you a horde of novel desserts in this book: **"Mousses, Cheesecakes & Cupcakes".**

Apart from widening your choice, the desserts covered in this book also come with an element of convenience, since they can be made in advance! However, making them needs a good amount of planning, understanding and practice. Do not fret; this book serves as a detailed guide, giving you instructions on every aspect—right from making the mousses, cheesecakes and cupcakes to decorating and presenting them. Just remember that the success of these recipes lies in following the procedure perfectly, and being meticulous while measuring the ingredients. Even a slight variation might land you with a messy dessert.

I have divided the book into three sections, namely, **Mousses, Cheesecakes and Cupcakes**. Each section has a brief introduction on the ingredients that go into the making of these luscious desserts along with pointers to be kept in mind while making them. A piece of advice from my side is to read these pointers carefully before making any of the recipes from this book.

The book begins with a section on Mousses, where I have presented 16 interesting options. So, what is so special about these? Worldwide, mousses are commonly made with egg as a setting ingredient. For my vegetarian readers, I have made these mousses comprising of either agar-agar or chocolate itself as a setting agent. From the evergreen **Chocolate Mousse**, page 10., and **Strawberry Mousse,** page 26, to the innovative **Coconut Pineapple Mousse**, page 14 and **Caramelized Apple Mousse**, page 20, there are umpteen delectable recipes to be enjoyed in this section. I have also shared a traditional mousse, the **Thandai Mousse**, page 24 to be enjoyed by the whole family.

The second section focuses on Cheesecakes, a class of desserts I love! Cheesecakes are crunchier when compared to other desserts like cakes, pastries, mousses or even cupcakes. The biscuit base of the cheesecakes is what makes it different from the others. With whipped cream, butter, fresh cream and cream cheese as basic ingredients, just a small portion of cheesecake can be quite satiating! All-time favourites like **Chocolate Cheesecake**, page 42, and **Blueberry Cheesecake**, page 44, are presented along with fruit-based cheesecakes like **Peach Cheesecake**, page 46, **Mango cheesecake**, page 50, etc.

Cupcakes, the third variety of dessert covered in this book, is indeed a very versatile one—it can be made as simple or as grand as you want. It is a very popular dessert option because it comes in small, easy-to-handle portions, and is quite simple to prepare. Thereafter, rich frostings with colourful garnishes can be used to add to its appeal. We have shown a few frosting ideas here, but you can use different kinds of nozzles to shape your frostings in varied ways. The garnishes can also be changed as per your choice. In short, you can start with a simple sponge and morph it into a delectable dessert with various frosting and garnishing ideas! **Oreo Cupcake**, page 58, **Chocolate Chip Cupcake**, page 66, and some unique combinations like **Cinnamon Cupcake**, page 60, and **Coffee walnut Cupcake**, page 70, feature in this section.

In short, this book will help you conjure up a dessert that diners will remember all night, and for all the days to come thereafter! Get going, win as many hearts as you can, and may people remember you as a chef par excellence.

Regards

Tarla Dalal

Index

Mousses

About Mousses

Cheesecakes

About Cheesecakes

Cupcakes

About Cupcakes

About Mousses

Mousse is a French word which means "lather" or "foam".

A mousse is a form of dessert typically made from egg and whipped cream, but in this book we have made eggless mousses by using whipped cream and china grass (*agar agar*).

The mousses are further enhanced with chocolates, fruits, dry fruits, essence and so on....
The use of right quality and proportion of ingredients are a very important key to its success. Lets discuss each of these in detail.

Commonly Used Ingredients for Mousses

1. Whipped Cream: There are 3 types of whipped creams available in the market like Rich's cream, Dairy cream and Powdered cream. The best results come with Rich's cream followed by dairy cream. If using powdered cream, follow the exact instructions on the packet. The cream available in tetra packs (like Amul, Vijaya etc.) is fresh cream and cannot be whipped at all and hence not suitable for making mousses.

Whipping the cream to its correct stage is very crucial to make mousses. **1¼ cups of whipped cream will approx. yield 2 cups of whipped cream and this will take approx. 8 to 10 minutes.** Always use an electric beater and not a hand beater to whip the cream. This whipped cream can be made in advance and stored in the refrigerator for 1 to 2 hours to save time. The adding of whipped cream to any other mixture and mixing it very gently is known as **"folding"**. This is best done only with the help of a rubber spatula.

2. Agar-agar : Agar-agar also known as China grass is a vegetable "gelatin" derived from a number of seaweeds which are processed by boiling and drying. Known as a vegetarian setting agent for mousses, it is available in the form of white, translucent, crinkly sheets. It has no flavour and a neutral taste. Use the correct proportion of agar-agar as mentioned in the recipes, since slight variations in the proportions may spoil the texture of the mousse. Always cut agar agar into small pieces before using them in the recipes. Straining the agar-agar mixture is very important to obtain a smooth mixture free of lumps.

3. Chocolate: A most common and preferred flavouring agent in mousses. It comes in varieties like dark chocolate, milk chocolate and white chocolate. A good chocolate is shiny brown, breaks clearly and free of lumps, tiny bursts and white specks.

When using chocolate in making mousses always grate or chop them as per the recipe. This will help in uniform and quick melting. After removing it from the microwave / gas ensure to whisk it gently to make it smooth. It should always be stored at room temperature, if you are storing it in a refrigerator during summer months make sure you bring it to room temperature before using it.

4. Essence : Essences are natural or artificial flavouring agents which are added to the batter / mixture towards the end. They should always be used very sparingly.

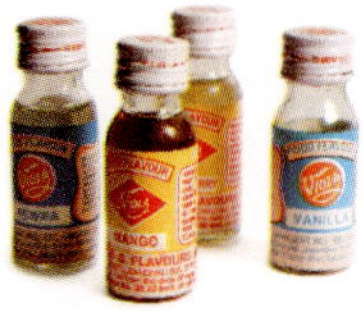

General Pointers for making Mousses

- Use measuring cups and spoons to get the perfect recipe.
- Keep all the ingredients measured before making the recipe.
- When using milk, use full-fat milk as it sets well.
- When using *paneer* it is best to use freshly made to get the perfect needed texture of the mousse.
- Always taste the sugar and lemon as they vary in all recipes.
- After making the mousse mixture pour them into glasses / bowls immediately else it may start setting lightly in the mixing bowl.
- Always set mousses in different glasses / bowls as you cannot demould them.
- When refrigerating the mousses, preferably keep them covered to avoid any spillage of water.
- Once the mousse is refrigerated to set, don't touch or shake it, as this tends to disturb the setting of the mousse.
- Always garnish the mousse just before serving.
- After the setting time most mousses stay fresh for 1 to 2 days.

Lemon Mousse

A delight that melts in your mouth and leaves an indelible mark of joy! This mousse is as light and soft as a soufflé, and has been made with paneer—an ingredient that you might not have thought of making mousses with before! The sharp lemon accent is the highlight of this recipe, both visually and taste-wise—and so, the use of lemon essence is very essential. The only thing you need to take care of is the balancing of sugar and lemon juice.

Preparation Time: 5 minutes. ■ Cooking Time: 8 to 10 minutes. ■ Serves 4. ■ Setting Time: 2 to 3 hours.

2 drops lemon yellow colour
1 tsp lemon rind
2 tsp lemon juice
1 drop lemon essence
¼ cup powdered sugar
¾ cup whipped cream, page 6

For the freshly made *paneer*
½ litre (2½ cups) full fat milk
1 tbsp lemon juice

To be blended into a smooth paste
½ cup freshly made *paneer* (cottage cheese), recipe above
½ cup milk
2 tbsp whipped cream, page 6

For the garnish
A few lemon drops
A few mint (*phudina*) sprigs
Lemon wedges

For the freshly made *paneer*
1. Bring the milk to boil in a deep pan.
2. When the milk starts boiling, remove from the flame, add the lemon juice and wait for 2 minutes.
3. Stir once and again wait for 2 minutes or till the milk is completely curdled. Strain it with the help of a strainer and squeeze out all the excess water from the *paneer.*
4. Keep aside and use as required.

How to proceed
1. Combine the lemon yellow colour, lemon rind, lemon juice, lemon essence, sugar and the prepared paste in a bowl and mix gently.
2. Add the whipped cream and fold gently.
3. Pour equal quantities of the mixture into 4 individual bowls / glasses and refrigerate for 2 to 3 hours or till the mousse sets.
4. Garnish it with lemon drops, mint sprigs and lemon wedges.
   Serve chilled.

Chocolate Mousse

Whether kids, teens or adults, almost everybody loves chocolate, and hence this mousse too! The luscious dark chocolate and the contrasting whipped cream together makes it a temptation hard to resist. What is more, this mousse is also one of the easiest to prepare. Just make sure that you use the right dark chocolate to ensure the best taste and colour. As far as possible, try not to store the chocolate in the fridge; else, bring it to room temperature before using in this recipe. Serve chilled with an elegant topping of whipped cream.

Preparation Time: 10 minutes. Cooking Time: 30 seconds. Serves 4. Setting Time: 2 to 3 hours.

1 cup roughly chopped dark chocolate
¼ cup milk
1 tbsp powdered sugar
1¾ cup whipped cream, page 6
¼ tsp vanilla essence
2 tsp honey

For the garnish
Grated chocolate

1. Combine the chocolate and milk in a microwave safe bowl and microwave on HIGH for 30 seconds. Remove and mix well until no lumps remain.
2. Strain the mixture using a sieve and keep aside.
3. Combine the sugar and ¾ cup whipped cream in a deep bowl and fold gently.
4. Add the chocolate–milk mixture and fold gently.
5. Add the vanilla essence and honey and fold gently.
6. Pour equal quantities of the mixture into 4 individual bowls / glasses and refrigerate for atleast 2 to 3 hours or till the mousse sets.
7. Top each bowl / glass with ¼ cup of whipped cream and garnish with chocolate and serve chilled.

Handy tip You can also melt the chocolate-milk mixture on a double boiler.

VARIATION:
Rich Mint Chocolate Mousse:
Add step 5, instead of vanilla essence add 2 tsp of peppermint essence, mix well and proceed as per the recipe.

Coffee Mousse

If chocolate mousse is for those who like the sweet and indulgent smell of cocoa, this mousse is for those who love the rich, invigorating aroma of coffee! Whip together a super combo of chocolate, milk and coffee powder and you will end up with a perfectly creamy mousse to romance with your taste buds. What is more, this mousse is also quite easy to make; and if you have a good quality coffee powder and the perfect decoction, you just cannot control the compliments!

Preparation Time: 5 minutes. **Cooking Time: 30 seconds.** **Serves 4.** **Setting Time: 3 to 4 hours.**

1 cup roughly chopped milk chocolate
¼ cup milk
1 tbsp powdered sugar
2½ cups whipped cream, page 6
1 tbsp coffee powder dissolved in 1 tbsp warm milk

For the garnish
Grated dark chocolate

1. Combine the chocolate and milk in a microwave safe bowl and microwave on HIGH for 30 seconds. Remove and mix well until no lumps remain.
2. Strain the mixture using a sieve and keep aside.
3. Combine the sugar and 1½ cups whipped cream in a deep bowl and fold gently.
4. Add the chocolate–milk mixture and fold gently.
5. Add the coffee mixture and fold gently.
6. Pour equal quantities of the mixture into 4 individual bowls / glasses and refrigerate for atleast 3 to 4 hours or till the mousse sets.
7. Top each bowl / glass with ¼ cup of whipped cream.
   Serve chilled garnished with grated chocolate .

Handy tip You can also melt the chocolate-milk mixture on a double boiler.

VARIATION:
Coffee Mousse on a Chocolate Biscuit Crust:
At step 5, before adding the mixture make a layer of biscuit crust in the bowls/glasses. To make this layer, combine 1 cup of coarsely crushed chocolate biscuits and 2 tbsp of melted butter in a bowl and mix well. Divide the crust into 4 equal portions and place equal quantities into 4 individual bowls / glasses and proceed as per the recipe.

Coconut Pineapple Mousse

Voila, the well-known Pinacolada combo has been transformed into a mousse! This delicious mousse, with its winning looks, is a popular one in Eastern countries and is sure to be liked by all who taste it. For best results, use readymade coconut milk. I would also suggest that you use canned pineapples to capitalise on their sweetness and softness—and to avoid the sour and raw feel of fresh pineapples.

- **Preparation Time: 10 minutes.**
- **Cooking Time: 10 to 12 minutes.**
- **Serves 4.**
- **Setting Time: 3 to 4 hours.**
- **Soaking Time: 30 minutes.**

1 cup coconut milk (*nariyal ka doodh*)
¼ cup chopped canned pineapple
2.5 gms *agar-agar* (china grass), blended into a smooth powder
4 tbsp sugar
1 tsp lemon juice
1 drop lemon yellow colour
1 cup whipped cream, page 6

For the garnish
4 cherries

1. Soak the *agar-agar* in ¼ cup of warm water for 30 minutes and keep aside.
2. Combine the pineapple and ½ tbsp of sugar in a bowl, mix well and keep aside.
3. Heat a pan, add the soaked agar-agar and cook it till the agar-agar dissolves completely.
4. Meanwhile, combine the remaining 3½ tbsp of sugar and coconut milk in another deep pan and bring to boil, while stirring continuously.
5. Add the *agar-agar* mixture to the coconut-milk mixture, mix well and cook on a slow flame for 2 to 3 minutes, while stirring continuously.
6. Remove from the flame and strain the mixture using a sieve.
7. Transfer the mixture into a bowl and place the bowl in a deep vessel filled with ice-cubes for 8 to 10 minutes or until the mixture cools and thickens. Whisk the mixture vigorously and continuously till it is in ice-cube vessel to avoid any lump formation.
8. Add the prepared pineapples, lemon juice and lemon yellow colour and mix gently.
9. Add the whipped cream and fold gently.
10. Pour equal quantities of the mixture into 4 individual bowls / glasses and refrigerate for atleast 3 to 4 hours or till the mousse sets.
    Garnish with a cherry and serve chilled.

Quick Orange Mousse

The vivid colour and tangy taste of oranges dominates this quick mousse. But, what makes this recipe a real topper is the way the vibrant orange sauce contrasts and complements the pleasant white chocolate and soothing whipped cream. Orange squash is better suited for this recipe than fresh orange juice, as it totally voids the risk of bitterness. As a variant, the orange sauce can also be used over vanilla ice-cream.

- **Preparation Time: 10 minutes.** ▪ **Cooking Time: 3 minutes 30 seconds.** ▪ **Serves 4.**
- **Setting Time: 3 to 4 hours.**

For the orange sauce
¼ cup orange squash, readily available
½ tbsp sugar
½ tbsp orange rind
1 tbsp cornflour dissolved in 1 tbsp water

Other ingredients
1 cup roughly chopped white chocolate
¼ cup milk
1 tbsp powdered sugar
1½ cups whipped cream, page 6
2 drops orange colour

For the garnish
A few orange wedges

For the orange sauce
Combine all the ingredients in a deep non–stick pan and cook on a medium flame for 2 to 3 minutes or till the sauce thickens, while stirring continuously. Remove from the flame and keep aside.

How to proceed
1. Combine the chocolate and milk in a microwave safe bowl and microwave on HIGH for 30 seconds. Remove and mix well until no lumps remain.
2. Strain the mixture using a sieve and keep aside.
3. Combine the sugar, whipped cream, orange sauce and orange colour in a deep bowl and fold gently.
4. Add the chocolate-milk mixture and fold gently.
5. Pour equal quantities of the mixture into 4 individual bowls / glasses and refrigerate for atleast 3 to 4 hours or till the mousse sets.
   Garnish with orange wedges and serve chilled.

Handy tip You can also melt the chocolate-milk mixture on a double boiler.

Mocha Cup

Are you game for a cupful of joy? Then, try this elegant dessert made from a perfect combination of coffee cream and chocolate mousse. The highlight of this dessert is its layered format, comprising chocolate mousse sandwiched between two layers of coffee mousse.

■ **Preparation Time: 10 minutes.** ■ **Cooking Time: 30 seconds.** ■ **Serves 4.** ■ **Setting Time: 2 to 3 hours.**

For the chocolate mousse
½ cup roughly chopped dark chocolate
2 tbsp milk
½ tbsp powdered sugar
⅓ cup whipped cream, page 6
¼ tsp vanilla essence
1 tsp honey

For the coffee cream
2 cups whipped cream, page 6
¼ cup powdered sugar
½ tsp vanilla essence
1 tbsp instant coffee powder dissolved in 1 tbsp warm water
2 tbsp melted dark chocolate

For the garnish
A few coffee beans

For the chocolate mousse

1. Combine the chocolate and milk in a microwave safe bowl and microwave on HIGH for 30 seconds. Remove and mix well till no lumps remain.
2. Strain the mixture using a sieve and keep aside.
3. Combine the powdered sugar and whipped cream in a deep bowl and fold gently.
4. Add the chocolate–milk mixture and fold gently.
5. Add the vanilla essence and honey and fold gently. Keep aside.

For the coffee cream

1. Combine the whipped cream, sugar and vanilla essence in a bowl and fold gently.
2. Add the coffee mixture and fold gently.
3. Add the melted chocolate and fold gently. Keep aside.

How to proceed

1. Pour the coffee cream into a plastic piping bag and fold the top end of the piping bag so as to seal it. Snip a bit off the tip so as to get a small hole for the piping to come out.
2. Pipe out $1/8$ of the coffee cream in a tall glass.
3. Pour the chocolate mousse into a plastic piping bag and fold the top end of the piping bag so as to seal it. Snip a bit off the tip so as to get a small hole for the piping to come out.
4. Pipe out ¼ of the chocolate mousse on top of the coffee cream in the same tall glass.
5. Again pipe out $1/8$ of the coffee cream on top of the chocolate mousse in the same tall glass.
6. Repeat the steps 2, 4 and 5 to make 3 more glasses.
7. Refrigerate for at least 2 to 3 hours or till the mousse sets.
8. Garnish with coffee beans and serve chilled.

Handy tip You can also melt the chocolate-milk mixture on a double boiler.

Caramelized Apple Mousse

This unique white chocolate mousse is sure to win every heart, especially those who are die-hard white chocolate fans! This recipe uses caramelised apples to enhance the looks and also to impart crunchiness to the mousse. For best results, make the caramelised apples just before serving. Apples can also be replaced with strawberries, pears, and other fruits that are in season.

- **Preparation Time: 10 minutes.**
- **Cooking Time: 10 minutes 30 seconds.**
- **Serves 4.**
- **Setting Time: 2 to 3 hours.**

For the white chocolate mousse

1 cup roughly chopped white chocolate
¼ cup milk
1 tbsp powdered sugar
1½ cups whipped cream, page 6
¼ tsp vanilla essence
½ tsp lemon juice

For the caramelized apples

12 apple slices
½ cup sugar

Other ingredients

1 cup roughly broken chocolate biscuits

For the white chocolate mousse

1. Combine the chocolate and milk in a microwave safe bowl and microwave on HIGH for 30 seconds. Remove from the microwave and mix well until no lumps remain.
2. Strain the mixture using a sieve. Keep aside.
3. Combine the sugar and whipped cream in a deep bowl and fold gently.
4. Add the chocolate–milk mixture and fold gently.
5. Add the vanilla essence and the lemon juice and fold gently.
6. Refrigerate for atleast 2 to 3 hours or till the mousse sets.

For the caramelized apples

1. Combine the sugar and ½ cup of water in a broad non-stick pan and cook till all the water evaporates and the sugar caramelizes (approx. 8 to 10 minutes).
2. Arrange 3 apple slices on a wooden stick and pour ¼ of the caramelized sugar immediately on them.
3. Repeat the step 2 to make 3 more caramelized apple sticks. Keep aside.

How to proceed

1. Place ¼ of the broken chocolate biscuit into 4 individual bowls/glasses.
2. Fill the plastic disposable piping bag fitted with a big star nozzle with the white mousse. Hold the piping bag in your hand and make your wrist anti-clockwise while applying gentle pressure to make few swirls one on top of each other on top of the crushed biscuits as shown in the image besides.

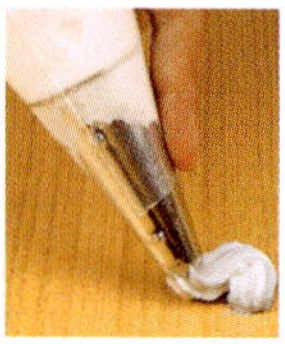

3. Place a caramelized apple stick on each glass / bowl.
   Serve immediately.

Handy tip You can also melt the chocolate-milk mixture on a double boiler.

Chocolate Banana Mousse

Chocolate and bananas are always a great combination—be it for a milkshakes, ice-creams, pastries or mousses! The bitterness of dark chocolate and the mild sweetness of bananas complement each other very well in this irresistible mousse. What is more, this fabulous dessert can be fixed up in no time at all!

Preparation Time: 10 minutes. **Cooking Time: 5 minutes.** **Serves 4.** **Setting Time: 2 to 3 hours.**

For the chocolate sauce
¾ cup roughly chopped dark chocolate
2 tbsp milk
2½ tbsp fresh cream

Other ingredients
½ cup mashed bananas
1 cup whipped cream, page 6
1 tsp powdered sugar
¼ tsp vanilla essence

For the garnish
4 banana wedges

For the chocolate sauce
1. Heat the milk and cream in a non-stick pan and bring to boil, while stirring continuously.
2. Remove from the flame, add the chocolate and mix gently to get a smooth mixture.
3. Cool to room temperature and keep aside.

How to proceed
1. Combine the bananas and the chocolate sauce in a bowl and mix gently.
2. Add the whipped cream, sugar and vanilla essence and fold gently.
3. Pour equal quantities of the mixture into 4 individual bowls / glasses and refrigerate for atleast 2 to 3 hours or till the mousse sets.

   Garnish with a banana wedge and serve chilled.

Handy tip To make the chocolate sauce in a microwave, combine all the ingredients in a microwave safe bowl and microwave on HIGH for 1 minute. Remove and mix well till no lumps remain.

Thandai Mousse

Here is a mousse with a desi dimension to it! Thandai mousse would be appropriate for occasions like Holi and other Indian festivals or get-togethers. The rich ingredients like almonds, khus-khus and cardamom that are present in the Thandai syrup give a slightly spicy touch to this mousse. This recipe uses readymade Thandai syrup, but in Rajasthan, the spices are ground freshly using a mortar and pestle every time Thandai is made..

Preparation Time: A few minutes. **Cooking Time: 5 to 7 minutes.** **Serves 4.**
Setting Time: 2 to 3 hours.

2 tbsp *thandai* syrup, readily available
5 gms *agar-agar* (china grass), blended into a smooth powder
1 cup milk
2 tbsp sugar
¾ cup whipped cream, page 6
½ tsp lemon juice

For the garnish
A few pistachios
A few saffron (*kesar*) strands

1. Combine the *agar-agar*, milk and ½ of cup water in a deep pan and bring to boil, while stirring continuously.
2. Add the *thandai* syrup and sugar, mix well and cook on a medium flame for 1 to 2 minutes, while stirring continuously.
3. Remove from the flame and strain the mixture using a sieve.
4. Transfer the mixture into a bowl and place the bowl in a deep vessel filled with ice-cubes for 8 to 10 minutes or until the mixture cools and thickens. Whisk the mixture vigorously and continuously till it is in ice-cube vessel to avoid any lump formation.
5. Add the whipped cream and lemon juice and fold gently.
6. Pour equal quantities of the mixture into 4 individual bowls / glasses and refrigerate for 2 to 3 hours or till the mousse sets.
   Garnished with pistachios and saffron and serve chilled.

Strawberry Mousse

Have you ever thought of combining red strawberries and fluffy soft paneer into an irresistible mousse? Although strawberries are seasonal, this mousse is surely worth a try when you can lay your hands on this juicy fruit. Here, the use of lemon juice is imperative as it brings out the full flavour of the strawberries. The paneer performs well as a setting agent to give just the right consistency to this mousse.

- **Preparation Time: 10 minutes.**
- **Cooking Time: 4 to 5 minutes.**
- **Serves 4.**
- **Setting Time: 2 to 3 hours.**

¼ cup chopped fresh strawberries
1 tsp of sugar
½ cup freshly made *paneer* (cottage cheese), page 8
½ cup milk
2 tbsp strawberry crush, readily available
1 tbsp powdered sugar
2.5 gms *agar-agar* (china grass), blended into a smooth powder
¾ tsp of lemon juice
1 cup whipped cream, page 6

For the garnish
A few chopped strawberries

1. Combine the strawberries and sugar in a bowl and mash gently using the back of a spoon. Keep aside.
2. Combine the *paneer*, 1 tbsp of milk, strawberry crush and sugar and blend in a mixer to a smooth purée. Keep aside.
3. Combine the *agar-agar*, remaining milk and ¼ cup of water in a deep pan and bring to boil, while stirring continuously.
4. Remove from the flame and strain the mixture using a sieve.
5. Transfer the mixture into a bowl and place the bowl in a deep vessel filled with ice-cubes for 8 to 10 minutes or until the mixture cools and thickens, whisk the mixture vigorously and continuously till it is in ice-cube vessel to avoid any lump formation.
6. Add the *paneer*-strawberry puree, mashed strawberries and lemon juice and mix well.
7. Add the whipped cream and fold gently.
8. Pour equal quantities of the mixture into 4 individual bowls / glasses and refrigerate for 3 to 4 hours or till the mousse sets.

   Garnish with strawberries and serve chilled.

Mango Ginger Mousse

The rather unusual combination of mangoes and ginger gives a unique and unbeatable flavour to this mousse. It is amazing how the shades of ginger, lemon and mint give a completely new look to the otherwise common mango dessert. Taste the mixture after adding all the ingredients, and balance the ginger and lemon flavours as per your individual preference.

- **Preparation Time: 5 minutes.**
- **Cooking Time: 5 to 7 minutes.**
- **Serves 4.**
- **Setting Time: 3 to 4 hours.**
- **Soaking Time: 15 minutes.**

1 cup Alphonso mango pulp
5 gms *agar-agar* (china grass), blended into a smooth powder
¼ cup milk
2½ tbsp sugar
1 tsp fresh ginger (*adrak*) juice
1 tsp lemon juice
1 tbsp finely crushed mint leaves (*phudina*)
1 cup whipped cream, page 6

For the garnish
A few mango slices
A few mint sprigs

1. Soak the *agar-agar* in ⅓ cup of warm water in a deep pan and keep aside for 15 minutes.
2. Add the mango pulp, milk and sugar in a deep pan, mix well and bring to boil, while stirring continuously.
3. Remove from the flame and strain the mixture using a sieve.
4. Transfer the mixture into a bowl and place the bowl in a deep vessel filled with ice-cubes for 8 to 10 minutes or until the mixture cools and thickens. Whisk the mixture vigorously and continuously till it is in ice-cube vessel to avoid any lump formation.
5. Add the ginger juice, lemon juice and mint leaves and mix well.
6. Add the whipped cream and fold gently.
7. Pour equal quantities of the mixture into 4 bowls / glasses and refrigerate for 3 to 4 hours or till the mousse sets.
   Garnish with mango slices and mint sprigs and serve chilled.

Handy tip For parties you can serve this mousse in chocolate tarts as shown in the image.

Chocolate Hazelnut Mousse

Crunchy, creamy, rich—there is no shortage of praise for this dessert! This is luscious party fare, with the special touch of hazelnuts. However, where hazelnuts are not available you can use walnuts instead, without compromising on the taste and feel. While making the praline, take care not to stir the sugar; allow it to melt on its own to avoid the sugar from sticking to the spatula. To make this mousse quick and easy, I have opted for a spread like Nutella that is readily available.

Preparation Time: 10 minutes. **Cooking Time: 10 minutes.** **Serves 4.** **Setting Time: 3 to 4 hours.**

For the hazelnut praline
½ cup coarsely chopped hazelnut
¼ cup castor sugar

Other ingredients
1 cup chopped dark chocolate
¼ cup milk
¾ cup chocolate hazelnut spread (*Nutella*), readily available
¼ tsp vanilla essence
1 tbsp powdered sugar
1½ cups whipped cream, page 6

For the garnish
Whipped cream
4 chocolate bytes

For the hazelnut praline
1. Melt the sugar in non-stick pan on a medium flame till it turns light brown in colour.
2. Add the hazelnuts and mix well to make a praline.
3. Pour the prepared mixture on the greased rolling board or butter paper and roll it with a greased rolling pin so as to get a thin layer.
4. Once set, crush the praline coarsely with a rolling pin and keep aside.

How to proceed
1. Combine the chocolate and milk in a microwave safe bowl and microwave on HIGH for 30 seconds. Remove from the microwave and mix well until no lumps remain.
2. Strain the mixture using a sieve and keep aside.
3. Add the chocolate hazelnut spread and vanilla essence and mix well.
4. Add the sugar and whipped cream and fold gently.
5. Add the prepared hazelnut praline and fold gently.
6. Pour equal quantities of the mixture into 4 individual bowls / glasses and refrigerate for atleast 3 to 4 hours or till the mousse sets.
   Garnish with whipped cream and a chocolate byte and serve chilled.

Handy tips
1. Instead of hazelnuts, you can use equal proportion of walnuts (*akhrot*).
2. You can also use milk chocolate instead of dark chocolate.
3. While making hazelnut praline, at step no. 4 do not touch the praline with your hand at this point as it is really hot and can cause serious burns.
4. You can also melt the chocolate-milk mixture on a double boiler.

White Chocolate Mousse
with Strawberry Sauce

Here is another interesting mousse that employs white chocolate. The specialty of this recipe is that it sets on its own, without any need for agar-agar. It is made with simple and easily available ingredients, making it ideal for any occasion. Fresh strawberry sauce tastes best, but when the fruit is not in season you can use strawberry crush; however, omit the sugar in that case to avoid over-sweetness.

- **Preparation Time: 10 minutes.**
- **Cooking Time: 5 minutes 30 seconds.**
- **Serves 4.**
- **Setting Time: 4 hours.**

For the white chocolate mousse
1 cup roughly chopped white chocolate
¼ cup milk
1 tbsp powdered sugar
1½ cups whipped cream, page 6
¼ tsp vanilla essence
½ tsp lemon juice

For the strawberry sauce
½ cup mashed strawberries
4 tsp sugar
½ tsp lemon juice
1 tsp cornflour
A few drops of cochineal (red colour)

For the white chocolate mousse
1. Combine the chocolate and milk in a microwave safe bowl and microwave on HIGH for 30 seconds. Remove from the microwave and mix well until no lumps remain.
2. Strain the mixture using a sieve and keep aside.
3. Combine the sugar and whipped cream in a deep bowl and fold gently.
4. Add the chocolate-milk mixture and fold gently.
5. Add the vanilla essence and the lemon juice and fold gently.
6. Pour equal quantities of the mixture into 4 individual bowls/glasses and refrigerate for 1 hour.

For the strawberry sauce
1. Combine all the ingredients along with ½ cup of water in a deep non-stick pan and cook for 4 to 5 minutes, while stirring continuously.
2. Remove from the flame and keep aside to cool completely.

How to proceed
Pour the cooled strawberry sauce over the prepared white chocolate mousse and refrigerate for 3 hours or till the mousse sets.
Serve chilled.

Handy tip You can also melt the chocolate-milk mixture on a double boiler.

Trio Mousse

Three types of chocolate in one lovely mousse, this is almost as elegant as a performance by three ballerinas! It is beautiful to look at, very creamy, and a delight for the most discerning of tongues. Being a 'trio', this should ideally be made with three types of chocolate, but in case you do not like any of the varieties, you can make three layers with just the two varieties that you like, by sandwiching one variety between two layers of another.

- **Preparation Time: 15 minutes.**
- **Cooking Time: 2 minutes 20 seconds.**
- **Serves 4.**
- **Setting Time: 3 to 4 hours.**

For the milk chocolate mousse
½ cup chopped milk chocolate
2 tbsp milk
½ tbsp powdered sugar
¾ cups whipped cream, page 6
⅛ tsp vanilla essence

For the white chocolate mousse
¼ cup roughly chopped white chocolate
1 tbsp milk
¼ tbsp powdered sugar
⅓ cup whipped cream, page 6
1 drop vanilla essence
2 drops lemon juice

For the chocolate mousse
½ cup roughly chopped dark chocolate
2 tbsp milk
½ tbsp powdered sugar
⅓ cup whipped cream, page 6
⅛ tsp vanilla essence
1 tsp honey

For the chocolate sauce
1 cup grated dark chocolate
¼ cup milk

For the milk chocolate mousse
1. Combine the chocolate and milk in a microwave safe bowl and microwave on HIGH for 30 seconds. Remove from the microwave and mix well until no lumps remain.
2. Strain the mixture using a sieve and keep aside.
3. Combine the sugar and whipped cream in a deep bowl and fold gently.
4. Add the chocolate-milk mixture and fold gently.
5. Add the vanilla essence and fold gently. Keep aside.

For the white chocolate mousse
1. Combine the chocolate and milk in a microwave safe bowl and microwave on HIGH for 30 seconds. Remove from the microwave and mix well until no lumps remain.
2. Strain the mixture using a sieve and keep aside.
3. Combine the sugar and whipped cream in a deep bowl and fold gently.
4. Add the chocolate-milk mixture and fold gently.
5. Add the vanilla essence and lemon juice and fold gently. Keep aside.

For the dark chocolate mousse
1. Combine the chocolate and milk in a microwave safe bowl and microwave on HIGH for 30 seconds. Remove from the microwave and mix well until no lumps remain.
2. Strain the mixture using a sieve and keep aside.
3. Combine the sugar and whipped cream in a deep bowl and fold gently.
4. Add the chocolate-milk mixture and fold gently.
5. Add the vanilla essence and honey and fold gently. Keep aside.

For the chocolate sauce

1. Combine the chocolate and milk in a microwave safe bowl and microwave on HIGH for 50 seconds.
2. Remove from the microwave and mix well until no lumps remain. Keep aside.

How to proceed

1. Pour the milk chocolate mousse into a plastic piping bag and fold the top end of the piping bag so as to seal it. Snip a bit off the tip so as to get a small hole for the piping to come out.
2. Pipe out ¼ of the milk chocolate mousse in a tall glass.
3. Pour the white chocolate mousse into a plastic piping bag and fold the top end of the piping bag so as to seal it. Snip a bit off the tip so as to get a small hole for the piping to come out.
4. Pipe out ¼ of the white chocolate mousse on top of the milk chocolate mousse in the same tall glass.
5. Pour the dark chocolate mousse into a plastic piping bag and fold the top end of the piping bag so as to seal it. Snip a bit off the tip so as to get a small hole for the piping to come out.
6. Pipe out ¼ of the dark chocolate mousse on top of the white chocolate mousse in the same tall glass.
7. Pour ¼ of the chocolate sauce and rotate the glass clockwise. So as to spread it evenly.
8. Repeat the steps 2, 4, 6 and 7 to make 3 more glasses.
9. Refrigerate for at least 3 to 4 hours or till the mousse sets.
   Serve chilled.

Handy tip You can also melt the chocolate-milk mixture on a double boiler.

Hot Chocolate Mousse

This wonderful mousse can be whipped up in less than two minutes using a microwave oven! It is hot, yummy, quick—what more can you ask for? You can prepare the mixture in advance, store it in individual serving bowls, and microwave it just before serving to enjoy the best flavour. For an extra celebration, serve the hot mousse with chilled vanilla ice-cream!

Preparation Time: 5 minutes. **Cooking Time: 1 minute 40 seconds.** **Serves 4.**

½ cup milk
2¼ tbsp cocoa powder
1 cup *paneer* (cottage cheese) cubes
6 tbsp sugar
1 tsp vanilla essence
2¼ tbsp plain flour (*maida*)
1 tsp baking powder
1½ tbsp fresh cream
2 tbsp grated dark chocolate

For the garnish
A few chopped walnuts (*akhrot*)

1. Combine all the ingredients, except the cream and the chocolate, and blend in a mixer to a smooth paste.
2. Transfer the mixture to a bowl, add the fresh cream and chocolate and fold gently.
3. Pour equal quantities of the mixture into 4 individual bowls of approx. 50 mm. (2") diameter.
4. Place all the 4 bowls in a microwave and microwave on HIGH for 1 minute 40 seconds.
   Serve immediately garnished with walnuts.

Blueberry Mousse

A tempting combination of white chocolate and blueberry crush, this is another easy-to-make mousse that you cannot resist! You would definitely have come across blueberry cheesecake, but this mousse might be quite new to you; so make sure you try it next time you host a party. A garnish of petite chocolate fans will improve the looks manifold, but if you find them difficult to make, you can garnish with a liberal helping of chocolate chips, chocolate shavings or blueberry crush.

- **Preparation Time: 5 minutes.**
- **Cooking Time: 30 seconds.**
- **Serves 4.**
- **Setting Time: 2 to 3 hours.**

3 tbsp blueberry crush
1 cup roughly chopped white chocolate
¼ cup milk
1 tbsp powdered sugar
1½ cups whipped cream, page 6
¼ tsp vanilla essence
½ tsp lemon juice

For the garnish

Chocolate fans, refer diagram

1. Combine the chocolate and milk in a microwave-safe bowl and microwave on HIGH for 30 seconds. Remove, mix well until no lumps remain.
2. Strain the mixture using a sieve and keep aside.
3. Combine the sugar and whipped cream in deep bowl and fold gently.
4. Add the chocolate-milk mixture and fold gently.
5. Add the vanilla essence, lemon juice and blueberry crush and fold gently.
6. Pour equal quantities of the mixture into 4 individual bowls/glasses and refrigerate for 2 to 3 hours or till the mousse sets. Garnish with chocolate fans and serve chilled.

Handy tip You can also melt the chocolate-milk mixture on a double boiler.

For the chocolate fans

1. To make chocolate fans, pour a little melted chocolate on a clean dry marble surface. Now spread the melted chocolate using a palate knife from left to right and viceversa 4 to 5 times to the temper the chocolate. Refer diagram 1. This is done to cool the melted chocolate slightly and also to give shine to the chocolate.

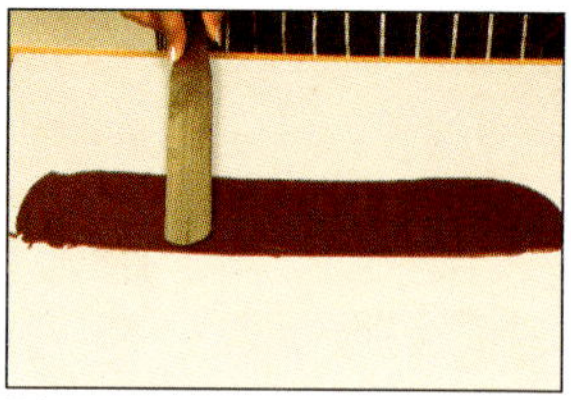

Diagram 1

2. With light pressure, run the dough cutter down the chocolate layer. You simply want to scrape off a small layer, not cut into the chocolate. As you are creating your fan shape, you can use your free hand to guide the strip of chocolate into gentle folds, waves, or a fan shape. Refer diagram 2. If your hands are very warm and start melting the chocolate, use thin plastic gloves. Use for garnish as required.

Diagram 2

About Cheesecakes

A creamy rich and incredibly versatile cheesecake is a most popular dessert. A cheesecake comprises of basic three components: a crust, a filling and a topping.

- **The crust :** The crust is the first and the base layer of the cheesecake. It is one of the most important layer as it holds the filling. Crushed biscuits are the most common base used. However sometimes sponge cakes are also used.
- **The filling :** This second layer of the cheesecake is the soft, creamy and rich. It is made by combining freshly made *paneer*, cream cheese, whipped cream, fruits, powdered sugar and essence.
- **The topping :** Right after being chilled, cheesecakes can be topped with various choices like whipped cream, fruits, chocolates or crushes.

Commonly Used Ingredients for Cheesecakes

1. **Biscuits :** Digestive and dark chocolate biscuits are the most common ones used as the base for cheesecakes. When using dark chocolate biscuits, remove and discard the middle creamy layer and use only the biscuits. Always crush the biscuits coarsely by using a rolling pin and not a mixer.

2. **Butter :** Combined with biscuits, it is used for the base of the cheesecakes. Always use melted butter in the recipes. Use the exact amount of butter mentioned in the recipe so as to form a firm crunchy base which does not break after setting.

3. **Sponge Cake :** When using sponge cakes for the crust, use readymade sponges to save on time. Sugar syrup plays an important role while using sponges as it moistens the cake and avoids them from being dry.

4. **Freshly made *Paneer* :** Full fat-milk curdled with lemon juice to make fresh *paneer* is used in the fillings of the cheesecakes. Freshly made *paneer* is important to get a smooth texture filling of the cheesecake.

5. **Whipped Cream:** There are 3 types of whipped creams available in the market like Rich's cream, Dairy cream and Powdered cream. The best results come with Rich's cream followed by dairy cream. If using powdered cream, follow the exact instructions on the packet. The cream available in tetra packs (like Amul, Vijaya etc.) is fresh cream and cannot be whipped at all and hence not suitable for making mousses.

Whipping the cream to its correct stage is very crucial to make mousses. **1¼ cups of whipped cream will approx. yields 2 cups of whipped cream and this will take approx. 8 to 10**

minutes. Always use an electric beater and not a hand beater to whip the cream. This whipped cream can be made in advance and stored in the refrigerator for 1 to 2 hours to save time. The adding of whipped cream to any other mixture and mixing it very gently is known as **"folding"**. This is best done only with the help of a rubber spatula.

6. **Cream Cheese :** Cheesecakes are made using Philadelphia or Mascarpone cheese usually. However since this isn't easily available and not very economical, we have used Amul cream cheese in the filling mixture. **This Amul cream cheese is combined with freshly made *paneer* and powdered sugar to improve on its texture. Always remember to strain this mixture to avoid grainy texture and make the filling smooth.**

7. **Powdered Sugar :** Granulated sugar blended in a mixer to a fine powder is powdered sugar. You can grind this at home or it is also readily available in the market.

General Pointers for making Cheesecakes

- Use measuring cups and spoons to get the perfect recipe.
- Keep all the ingredients measured before making the recipe.
- Only use a round loose bottom tin for setting cheesecakes.
- When using milk, use full-fat milk as it sets well.
- Always taste the sugar and lemon as they vary in all recipes.
- Spread the base mixture in the tin i.e. crust and then ensure to pat the mixture with the help of your fist so as to form a perfect uniform layer.
- Similarly after spreading the filling mixture finish it evenly using a palate knife.
- When fruits are used in the filling of the cheesecakes, consume it within 3 to 4 hours of making as prolonged time leads to release of water thus making the cheesecake soggy and also sour in taste.
- Once the cheesecake is refrigerated to set, don't touch or shake it, as this tends to disturb the setting of the cheesecake.
- When refrigerating the cheesecake, preferably keep them covered to avoid any spillage of water.
- If the cheesecake has been refrigerated for a long time and the base of the tin doesn't loosen easily, rotate the entire tin on a slow open flame of the gas very gently for 15 to 20 seconds. This will help loosen the sides of the cheesecake.
- Always finish the last layer of the cheesecake viz. topping/garnish after demoulding just before serving.
- To get smooth finished cheesecake wedges, cut the cheesecake with the help of a big knife after immersing it in warm water. This should be done for cutting every wedge to get clean wedges.

Chocolate Cheesecake

Show off your culinary skills by making this superb dessert. Don't set yourself worrying though, because this is quite easy to make. The secret behind this cheesecake is the use of good quality dark chocolate, and melting the chocolate for the right span of time only. Even a slight variation in the melting time will cause the chocolate to get burnt and spoil the texture of the mixture. You can add to the specialty of this cheesecake by using chocolate biscuits with a touch of rum as a base.

Preparation Time: 15 minutes. **Cooking Time: 10 to 12 minutes.** **Makes 1 cheesecake (6 wedges).** **Setting Time: 2 hour.**

For the biscuit base

24 digestive biscuits
½ cup melted butter

For the basic cheesecake

1 litre (5 cups) milk
2 tbsp lemon juice
6 tbsp powdered sugar
2 tbsp cream cheese, readily available

For the chocolate ganache

¾ cup grated dark chocolate
½ cup fresh cream

Other ingredients

2 cups roughly chopped dark chocolate
½ cup fresh cream
1 tsp vanilla essence
1 cup whipped cream, page 40

For the garnish

White and dark chocolate squares
White chocolate triangles
White chocolate vermicelli

For the biscuit base

1. Place the biscuits on a butter paper or a rolling board and crush to a coarse powder with the help of a rolling pin.
2. Transfer the crushed biscuit powder to a bowl, add the butter and mix well.
3. Spread and press the mixture into the base of a 175 mm. (7") loose bottomed cake tin.
4. Refrigerate for 10 minutes. Keep aside.

For the basic cheesecake

1. Keep 4 tbsp of milk aside and boil the remaining milk in a deep pan.
2. When the milk starts boiling, remove from the flame and add the lemon juice and wait for 2 minutes.
3. Stir once and again wait for 2 minutes or till the milk is completely curdled, strain it with the help of a strainer and squeeze out all the excess water from the *paneer*.
4. Combine the prepared *paneer*, 4 tbsp milk (kept aside) and sugar and blend in a mixer to a smooth paste.
5. Transfer the paste into a bowl, add the cream cheese and mix well.
6. Strain the prepared mixture with the help of a sieve and keep aside.

For the chocolate ganache

1. Heat the cream in a non-stick pan and bring to boil, while stirring continuously.
2. Remove from the flame, add the chocolate and mix gently to get a smooth mixture.
3. Cool to room temperature and keep aside.

How to proceed

1. Combine the chocolate and fresh cream in a deep microwave safe bowl and microwave on HIGH for 50 seconds. Remove from the microwave and mix gently till no lumps remain.
2. Strain the chocolate-cream mixture using a sieve.
3. Add the vanilla essence and mix well.
4. Add the basic cheesecake mixture and mix well.

5. Add the whipped cream and fold gently.
6. Pour this mixture evenly on the prepared biscuit base and spread it evenly using a palate knife.
7. Refrigerate for 1 hour or till the cheesecake sets.
8. Once it is set, pour the chocolate ganache on the cheesecake and spread it evenly using a palate knife. Again refrigerate for 1 hour.
9. Demould the cheesecake and garnish with white and dark chocolate squares, white chocolate triangles and vermicelli.
10. Cut into 6 equal wedges and serve chilled.

Blueberry Cheesecake

If you want to please a special person on a special occasion, this is the right dessert to pick! A firm cheesecake finished with a sweet blueberry topping, this is a truly satisfying experience. It is quite exotic and different from other cheesecakes that make use of biscuits as a base—as this cheesecake uses soft luscious vanilla sponge. Since blueberries are not readily available in India, you can use blueberry crush, without changing the total effect in any way.

Preparation Time: 15 minutes. **Cooking Time: 10 to 12 minutes.** **Makes 1 cheesecake (6 wedges).** **Setting Time: 4 hours.**

For the base

1¼ cups crumbled vanilla sponge, readily available
2 tbsp sugar syrup, refer handy tip

For the basic cheesecake

1 litre (5 cups) milk
2 tbsp lemon juice
5 tbsp powdered sugar
¼ cup fresh cream
2 tbsp cream cheese, readily available

Other ingredients

¼ cup blueberry crush, readily available
1 tsp lemon juice
1 cup whipped cream, page 40

For the garnish

8 tbsp blueberry crush

For the base

1. Spread and press the sponge cake into the base of a 175 mm. (7") loose bottomed cake tin.
2. Soak the sponge cake layer with the sugar syrup and keep aside.

For the basic cheesecake

1. Keep 4 tbsp of milk aside and boil the remaining milk in a deep pan.
2. When the milk starts boiling, remove from the flame, add the lemon juice and wait for 2 minutes.
3. Stir once and again wait for 2 minutes or till the milk is completely curdled. Strain it with the help of a strainer and squeeze out all the excess water from the *paneer.*
4. Combine the prepared *paneer*, 4 tbsp milk (kept aside), sugar and fresh cream and blend in a mixer to a smooth paste.
5. Transfer the paste into a bowl, add the cream cheese and mix well.
6. Strain the prepared mixture with the help of a sieve and keep aside.

How to proceed

1. Combine the basic cheesecake mixture, blueberry crush and lemon juice in a bowl and mix well.
2. Add the whipped cream and fold gently.
3. Pour this mixture evenly over the prepared sponge cake base and spread it evenly using a palate knife.
4. Refrigerate for 1 hour or till the cheesecake sets.
5. Pour the blueberry crush over the cheesecake and spread it evenly using a palate knife.
6. Demould the cheesecake, cut into 6 equal wedges and serve chilled.

Handy tips

1. To make 2 tbsp of sugar syrup, combine 2 tbsp of sugar with ½ tbsp of water in a small saucepan and allow to simmer on a slow flame till the sugar thickens.
2. For parties, you can set the cheesecake into individual moulds of your choice.

Peach Cheesecake

This recipe offers a sophisticated twist to traditional cheesecakes! It adds the deep, special touch of a dark chocolate biscuit base and a chocolate chip cheesecake mixture to the mellow caramelised peaches. It would be good to use tinned peaches for this recipe rather than fresh ones, because the former offers the best balance of sweetness, sourness and softness.

- **Preparation Time: 5 minutes.**
- **Cooking Time: 10 minutes.**
- **Makes 1 cheesecake (6 wedges)**
- **Setting Time: 6 to 7 hours.**

For the biscuit base

14 dark chocolate biscuits
3 tbsp melted butter

For the peach sauce

1½ tbsp sugar
¾ cup sugar syrup (from the can of tinned peaches)
1 tsp cornflour dissolved in 1 tsp of water
1 tbsp melted chocolate
6 to 7 tinned peach halves

Other ingredients

1 recipe basic cheesecake, page 42
2 tbsp chocolate chips
1½ cups whipped cream, page 40

For the biscuit base

1. Open each dark chocolate biscuit and scrape and discard the middle creamy layer.
2. Place the biscuits on a butter paper or a rolling board and crush to a coarse powder with the help of a rolling pin.
3. Transfer the crushed biscuit powder to a bowl, add the butter and mix well.
4. Spread and press the mixture into the base of a 175 mm. (7") loose bottomed cake tin.
5. Refrigerate for 10 minutes and keep aside.

For the peach sauce

1. Combine the sugar with 1½ tsp of water in a non-stick pan and cook till the sugar caramelizes and turns brown in colour.
2. Add the peach syrup, cornflour mixture, melted chocolate, mix well and simmer for 5 minutes.
3. Add the peach halves, mix well and simmer further for 2 minutes.
4. Remove from the flame and keep aside to cool.

How to proceed

1. Combine the basic cheesecake mixture and chocolate chips in a bowl and mix well.
2. Add the whipped cream and fold gently.
3. Pour this mixture evenly on the biscuit base and spread it evenly with the help of a palate knife.
4. Refrigerate for 6 to 7 hours or till the cheesecake sets.
5. Demould the cheesecake, arrange the peach halves on the cheesecake and pour the sauce over it.
6. Cut into 6 equal wedges and serve chilled.

Kiwi Cheesecake

Ah, the layers of this cheesecake get better and better—from the crumbly buttery biscuit base to the soft cheesecake in the middle, to the lemony kiwi glaze on top. Use properly ripe kiwis to get the perfect taste and avoid the sourness. In case kiwis are not available or not to your taste, you can substitute it with cherries or strawberries.

- **Preparation Time: 10 minutes.**
- **Cooking Time: 5 minutes.**
- **Makes 1 cheesecake (6 wedges).**
- **Setting Time: 4 hours.**

For the biscuit base
14 dark chocolate biscuits
3 tbsp melted butter

For the kiwi glaze
3 tbsp sugar
1 tsp cornflour
¾ tbsp lemon juice
½ tsp grated lemon rind
2 drops lemon essence
½ tsp butter
¾ cup thinly sliced kiwis

Other ingredients
1 recipe basic cheesecake, page 42
¼ cup finely chopped kiwis
½ tsp lemon essence
½ tsp lemon juice
1½ cups whipped cream, page 40

For the biscuit base
1. Open each dark chocolate biscuit and scrape and discard the middle creamy layer.
2. Place the biscuits on a butter paper or a rolling board and crush to a coarse powder with the help of a rolling pin.
3. Transfer the crushed biscuit powder to a bowl, add the butter and mix well.
4. Spread and press the mixture into the base of a 175 mm. (7") loose bottomed cake tin.
5. Refrigerate for 10 minutes and keep aside.

For the kiwi glaze
1. Combine all the ingredients, except the kiwis, in a deep non-stick pan and bring to boil, while stirring continuously.
2. Strain the sauce using a sieve and keep aside to cool.
3. Add the kiwis, mix well and keep aside.

How to proceed
1. Combine the basic cheesecake mixture, kiwis, lemon essence and lemon juice in a bowl and mix well.
2. Add the whipped cream and fold gently.
3. Pour this mixture over the biscuit base and spread it evenly using a palate knife.
4. Refrigerate for 4 hours or till the cheesecake sets.
5. Arrange the glazed kiwis evenly over it and keep refrigerated for at least 10 to 15 minutes or till the glaze is firm.
6. Demould the cheesecake, cut into 6 equal wedges and serve chilled.

Mango Cheesecake

Here is another yummy cheesecake with a soft vanilla sponge base. The tangy flavour of mango goes well with the mild vanilla-flavoured base. This recipe can be made throughout the year as it uses readymade mango pulp instead of fresh fruit. However, when the season is in full bloom, you can use fresh Alphonso mangoes for garnishing—this will surely make the recipe all the more special! However, avoid other fruits or canned mangoes as these will not taste good.

- **Preparation Time: 10 minutes.**
- **Cooking Time: Nil.**
- **Makes 1 cheesecake (6 wedges).**
- **Setting Time: 4 hours.**

For the base
1¼ cups crumbled vanilla sponge cake, readily available
2 tbsp sugar syrup, refer handy tip

Other ingredients
1 recipe basic cheesecake, page 42
½ cup mango pulp, readily available
½ cup whipped cream, page 40

For the garnish
2 cups mango slices

For the base
1. Spread and press the sponge cake into the base of a 175 mm. (7") loose bottomed cake tin.
2. Soak the sponge cake layer with the sugar syrup and keep aside.

How to proceed
1. Combine the basic cheesecake mixture and mango pulp in a bowl and mix well.
2. Add the whipped cream and fold gently.
3. Pour this mixture over the sponge cake base and spread it evenly using a palate knife.
4. Refrigerate for 4 hours or till the cheesecake sets.
5. Demould the cheesecake and place the mango slices all over the cheesecake overlapping each other.
6. Cut into 6 equal wedges and serve chilled.

Handy tip To make 2 tbsp of sugar syrup, combine 2 tbsp of sugar with ½ tbsp of water in a small saucepan and allow to simmer on a slow flame till the sugar thickens.

Strawberry Cheesecake

The crispy biscuit base laden with fresh and creamy fruits is sure to excite even the most tired taste buds! Quite naturally, this is one of the most popular cheesecakes across the world, and there are many ways of making this international favourite. This particular version combines strawberries with white chocolate. You can even use a basic cheesecake mixture (page 42) instead, for an equally good experience. Depending on the sweetness of the strawberries, adjust the proportion of sugar in the strawberry sauce.

- **Preparation Time: 10 to 15 minutes.**
- **Cooking Time: 5 to 7 minutes.**
- **Makes 1 cake (6 wedges).**
- **Setting Time: 5 hours.**

For the biscuit base
16 digestive biscuit
¼ cup melted butter

For the strawberry sauce
½ cup mashed strawberries
3 tbsp sugar
1 tsp cornflour
½ tsp lemon juice

Other ingredients
1 cup grated white chocolate
¼ cup milk
2 tbsp cream cheese, readily available
1 tsp lemon juice
1 tsp vanilla essence
1 cup whipped cream, page 40

Other ingredients
¾ cup sliced strawberries

For the garnish
¼ cup grated white chocolate

For the biscuit base
1. Place the biscuits on a butter paper or a rolling board and crush to a coarse powder with the help of a rolling pin.
2. Transfer the crushed biscuit powder to a bowl, add the butter and mix well.
3. Spread and press the mixture into the base of a 175 mm. (7") loose bottomed cake tin.
4. Refrigerate for 10 minutes and keep aside.

For the strawberry sauce
1. Combine all the ingredients along with ½ cup of water in a non-stick pan and bring to boil, while stirring continuously.
2. Strain the sauce using a sieve and keep aside to cool.

How to proceed
1. Combine the chocolate and milk in a microwave safe bowl and microwave on HIGH for 30 seconds. Remove from the microwave and mix gently till no lumps remain.
2. Add the cream cheese, mix gently and strain the mixture with the help of a strainer.
3. Transfer the chocolate-cream cheese mixture into a big bowl, add the lemon juice and vanilla essence and mix well.
4. Add the whipped cream and fold gently.
5. Pour this mixture evenly over the biscuit base and spread it evenly using a palate knife.
6. Refrigerate for at least 4 hours or till the cheesecake sets
7. Pour the strawberry sauce on the cheesecake and spread it evenly using a palate knife. Again refrigerate for 1 hour.
8. Demould the cheesecake, arrange the strawberry slices along the side and garnish with white chocolate along the circumference on the cheesecake.
9. Cut into 6 equal wedges and serve chilled.

Lemon Cheesecake

This is another popular cheesecake, commonly available in patisseries across the globe. The chocolate base combines superbly with the tanginess of lemon, making this as much of a connoisseur's delight as it is a child's treat. One thing you need to take care of is the perfect lemon rind for the perfect taste. Do not grate the lemon rind till its core; use only the yellow part and not the white. Before spreading the lemony sauce on the cheesecake, you can also spread a layer of fresh soft fruits of your choice.

- **Preparation Time: 10 minutes.**
- **Cooking Time: 5 to 7 minutes.**
- **Makes 1 cheesecake (6 wedges).**
- **Setting Time: 6 hours.**

For the biscuit base

14 chocolate biscuits
3 tbsp melted butter

For the lemon sauce

3 tbsp sugar
1 tsp cornflour dissolved in 2 tbsp of water
½ tsp butter
¾ tbsp lemon juice
½ tsp grated lemon rind
2 drops lemon essence
A drop of lemon yellow colour (optional)

Other ingredients

1 recipe basic cheesecake, page 42
2 tsp lemon juice
1 tsp grated lemon rind
½ cup powdered sugar
½ tsp lemon essence
1½ cups whipped cream, page 40

For the garnish

Lemon rind

For the biscuit base

1. Open each dark chocolate biscuit and scrape and discard the middle creamy layer.
2. Place the biscuits on a butter paper or a rolling board and crush to a coarse powder with the help of a rolling pin.
3. Transfer the crushed biscuit powder to a bowl, add the butter and mix well.
4. Spread and press the mixture into the base of a 175 mm. (7") loose bottomed cake tin.
5. Refrigerate for 10 minutes and keep aside.

For the lemon sauce

1. Combine the sugar with ½ cup of water in a non-stick pan and cook till the sugar dissolves.
2. Add the cornflour mixture, mix well and cook till the mixture thickens and gets a coating consistency, while stirring continuously.
3. Add the butter and mix well.
4. Remove from the flame allow to cool.
5. Add the lemon juice, lemon rind, lemon essence and lemon yellow colour and mix well. Keep aside till it cools completely.

How to proceed

1. Combine the basic cheesecake mixture, lemon juice, lemon rind, sugar and lemon essence in a bowl and mix well till it is smooth.
2. Add the whipped cream and fold gently.
3. Pour this mixture evenly over the prepared biscuit base and spread it evenly using a palate knife.
4. Refrigerate for 4 hours or till the cheesecake is firm.
5. Pour the lemon sauce evenly over it and spread it evenly using a palate knife.
6. Refrigerate again for 2 hours or till the cheesecake sets.
7. Demould the cheesecake and cut into 6 equal wedges.
8. Garnish each wedge with a lemon rind and serve chilled.

Handy tip For parties, you can set the cheesecake into individual moulds of your choice.

About Cupcakes

Cupcakes are small sweet individual sponge cakes baked in cup-shaped containers and hence the name. They are typically topped with a variety of icings, frostings and garnishes. The containers in which they are baked used to be muffin tins in olden days which have now been replaced with individual aluminium moulds, silicon moulds or paper cups. They are best designed to serve individual person.

Cupcakes are a favourite for parties and especially for children's parties, when they can be decorated with icing and sweets.

Cupcakes Comprises of 3 parts, they are: the sponge, the frosting and the garnish

- **The sponge :** As mentioned earlier, sponge cakes here are made in individual sizes. They can be of different flavours such as vanilla, chocolate, vanilla cinnamon, chocolate almond and so on....
- **The frosting :** The most important and this is what makes it different from muffins. It is made using butter and icing sugar as the key ingredients.
- **The garnish :** These are mainly for enhancing eye appeal and make them more attractive.

Commonly Used Ingredients for Cupcakes

1. **Maida :** Known as refined or plain flour, its gluten content is comparatively low which helps to hold the air bubbles evenly in the sponge batter thus giving firmness and soft texture to the sponge.

2. **Condensed Milk :** It's basically milk from which water has been removed and sugar has been added to yield a thick and sweet product. This avoids the use of sugar in making sponges.

3. **Icing Sugar :** It's a finely powdered sugar which because of its fine texture blends very perfectly in sponges. As it dissolves quickly without heating, it is a crucial ingredient for frostings.

4. **Butter :** Combined with icing sugar, it is used for making frostings to impart creaminess.

5. **Essence :** Essences are natural or artificial flavouring agents which are added to the sponge batter and frostings. They should always be used very sparingly.

General Pointers for making Cupcakes

- ➢ Use measuring cups and spoons to get the perfect recipe.
- ➢ Keep all the ingredients measured before making the recipe.
- ➢ Sieve the plain flour (*maida*) 2 to 3 times before making the sponge.

- Always use melted butter for making the sponge but room temperature butter for the frostings.
- Use the exact amount of butter mentioned in the recipe so as to form a firm but soft sponge.
- While making the batter for the sponge the ingredients should be mixed very gently.
- Grease the moulds or paper cups very well.
- When using paper cups preferably use 2 paper cups together so that the paper cups hold the weight of the sponge batter and also let them rise well.
- If your cupcakes are sticking to the moulds or paper cups, the problem could be that you haven't baked them long enough. Try increasing your baking time a little bit.
- Before you decorate cupcakes with frostings and garnishes, it is important to allow them to cool completely by removing them from the baking sheet or tin, and placing on a wire rack.
- Do not make the frosting mixture in advance. If kept at room temperature it might melt and if refrigerated it has a tendency to harden because of the use of butter. However if you plan to make the frosting mixture in advance, it is advisable to pipe out the frosting on the sponge and then refrigerate the cupcakes till served.
- Garnish the cupcakes just before serving.

Oreo Cupcake

Oreo is a household name all over the world—and these chocolaty, chocolaty biscuits are now commonly available in India too. This treat combines a rich, velvety chocolate cupcake with a yummy, buttery icing that comprises coarsely-powdered Oreo biscuits as a key ingredient. It is a perfect choice for birthday parties, kitty parties and high-tea parties.

■ Preparation Time: 5 minutes. ■ Cooking Time: Nil. ■ Makes 6 cupcakes.
■ Baking Temperature and Time: 200°C (400°F) for 10 minutes. ■ 180°C (360°F) for 15 to 20 minutes.

For the chocolate sponge (makes 6)
½ cup plain flour (*maida*)
2 tbsp cocoa powder
½ tsp baking powder
¼ tsp soda bi-carb
½ cup condensed milk
3 tbsp melted butter
½ tsp vanilla essence

For the frosting
6 Oreo biscuits
6 tbsp butter (at room temperature)
12 tbsp icing sugar
1 tsp vanilla essence

For the garnish
1½ Oreo biscuits, cut into quarters

For the chocolate sponge
1. Sieve the plain flour, cocoa powder, baking powder and soda bi-carb together in a bowl and keep aside.
2. Combine the condensed milk, butter, vanilla essence and approx. 1½ tbsp of water in another bowl and whisk well.
3. Add the flour mixture and fold gently with help of a spatula to make a batter of dropping consistency.
4. Pour equal quantity of the batter into 6 greased and dusted 68 mm. (2½") diameter aluminum moulds.
5. Bake in a pre-heated oven at 200°C (400°F) for 5 minutes and then at 180°C (360°F) for 15 to 20 minutes or till done. The sponge is done when it leaves the sides of the mould and is springy to touch.
6. Allow it to cool completely (approx. 30 minutes). Keep aside.

For the frosting
1. Open each oreo biscuit and scrape and discard the middle creamy layer. You will need only the biscuits for this recipe.
2. Place the biscuits on a butter paper or on a rolling board and crush them coarsely using a rolling pin. Keep aside.
3. Put the butter in a deep bowl and beat it using a spatula.
4. Add the icing sugar and mix well.
5. Add the coarsely powdered biscuits and vanilla essence, mix well and keep aside.

How to proceed
1. Fill the frosting in a piping bag as shown on page 20 and pipe out swirls of your choice on each cupcake.
2. Garnish each cupcake with a quarter piece of Oreo biscuit and serve immediately.

Cinnamon Cupcake

A spicy frosting on a vanilla cupcake, this is a gourmet preparation perfect for a fine audience. Those who like the sweet aroma of cinnamon are sure to go ga-ga over this luscious cupcake that echoes the wonders of this spice in every bite. Top it with nice colourful garnishes like edible balls and stars, and serve with flair at tea-time.

Preparation Time: 5 minutes. **Cooking Time: Nil.** **Makes 6 cupcakes.**
Baking Temperature and Time: 200°C (400°F) for 15 minutes. **150°C (300°F) for 15 to 20 minutes.**

For the vanilla cinnamon sponge
¾ cup plain flour (*maida*)
¾ tsp baking powder
¼ tsp soda bi-carbonate
2 tsp cinnamon (*dalchinni*) powder
½ cup (200 gms) condensed milk
3 tbsp melted butter
½ tsp vanilla essence

For the frosting
6 tbsp butter (at room temperature)
12 tbsp icing sugar
1½ tsp cinnamon (*dalchini*) powder (optional)

For the garnish
Edible coloured balls

For the vanilla cinnamon sponge
1. Sieve the plain flour, baking powder, soda bi-carb and cinnamon powder together in a bowl and keep aside.
2. Combine the condensed milk, melted butter, vanilla essence and approx. 2 tbsp of water in another bowl and whisk well.
3. Add the flour mixture and fold gently with help of a spatula to make a batter of dropping consistency.
4. Pour equal quantity of the batter into 6 greased and dusted 68 mm. (2½") diameter aluminum moulds.
5. Bake in a pre-heated oven at 200°C (400°F) for 10 minutes and then at 150°C (300°F) for 15 to 20 minutes or till done. The sponge is done when it leaves the sides of the mould and is springy to touch.
6. Allow it to cool completely (approx. 30 minutes). Keep aside.

For the frosting
1. Put the butter in a deep bowl and beat it using a spatula.
2. Add the icing sugar and cinnamon powder and mix well. Keep aside.

How to proceed
1. Fill the frosting in a piping bag as shown on page 20 and pipe out peaks or swirls of your choice on each cupcake.
2. Garnish each cupcake with edible coloured balls and serve immediately.

Peppermint Cupcake

A lively combo of cocoa and mint, this cupcake is a great way to share your joy with family and friends. Served with delicious peppermint ice-cream, it is ideal as an after-dinner treat for adults. For a stronger mint flavour, add a drop of peppermint essence to the chocolate cupcake batter before baking.

Preparation Time: A few minutes. **Cooking Time: Nil.** **Makes 6 cupcakes.**

6 chocolate sponge, page 58

For the frosting
6 tbsp butter (at room temperature)
12 tbsp icing sugar
6 tsp cocoa powder
1 tsp vanilla essence
1 tsp peppermint essence

For the frosting

1. Put the butter in a deep bowl and beat it using a spatula.
2. Add the icing sugar, cocoa powder, vanilla essence and peppermint essence and mix well. Keep aside.

How to proceed
Fill the frosting in a piping bag as shown on page 20 and pipe out swirls of your choice on each cupcake.
Serve immediately.

Mava Cupcake

Why think of cupcakes as a typically western format of cooking? Here is a version that is steeped in Indian tradition, made with readymade mava pedas. The hint of nutmeg adds to the desi character of this cupcake. For best results, use the freshest pedas, and serve with hot tea or coffee.

Preparation Time: 5 minutes. Cooking Time: Nil. Makes 6 cupcakes.
Baking Temperature and Time: 200°C (400°F) for 15 minutes. 150°C (300°F) for 15 to 20 minutes.

¾ cup plain flour (*maida*)
¾ tsp baking powder
¼ tsp soda bi-carbonate
½ cup (200 gms) condensed milk
3 tbsp melted butter
½ tsp vanilla essence
3 tbsp crumbled *mava (khoya) pedas*, readily available
2 tsp nutmeg (*jaiphal*) powder

For the garnish
Icing sugar
Nutmeg (*jaiphal*) powder
Edible coloured stars

1. Sieve the plain flour, baking powder and soda bi-carb together in a bowl and keep aside.
2. Combine the condensed milk, melted butter, vanilla essence and approx. 2 tbsp of water in another bowl and whisk well.
3. Add the flour mixture, *mava pedas* and nutmeg powder and mix gently with help of a spatula to make a batter of dropping consistency.
4. Pour equal quantity of the batter into 6 greased and dusted 68 mm. (2½") diameter aluminum moulds.
5. Bake in a pre-heated oven at 200°C (400°F) for 10 minutes and at 150°C (300°F) for 15 to 20 minutes or till done. The cupcake is done when it leaves the sides of the mould and is springy to touch.
6. Allow it to cool completely (approx. 30 minutes). Keep aside.
7. For the garnish, dust a little icing sugar and nutmeg powder evenly on top of each cupcake with the help of small strainer.
8. Finish it with a few edible coloured stars and serve immediately.

Chocolate Chip Cupcake

If the peppermint cupcake is ideal for adults, then the chocolate chip cupcake is best-suited for kids—and for adults who are young at heart! Children are sure to love this cupcake, where delicious chocolate chips play hide-and-seek. This cupcake has an unusual combo of both vanilla and chocolate flavours, and a fantastic butter icing with melted chocolate. You can make it even more appealing by garnishing with edible silver balls.

Preparation Time: 5 minutes. **Cooking Time: Nil.** **Makes 6 cupcakes.**
Baking Temperature and Time: 200°C (400°F) for 15 minutes. **150°C (300°F) for 15 to 20 minutes.**

For the vanilla chocolate chip sponge
¾ cup plain flour (*maida*)
¾ tsp baking powder
¼ tsp soda bi-carbonate
½ cup (200 gms) condensed milk
3 tbsp melted butter
½ tsp vanilla essence
2 tbsp chocolate chips

For the frosting
6 tbsp butter (at room temperature)
12 tbsp icing sugar
3 tbsp melted chocolate

For the garnish
Chocolate chips
Edible silver balls

For the vanilla chocolate chip sponge
1. Sieve the plain flour, baking powder and soda bi-carb together in a bowl and keep aside.
2. Combine the condensed milk, melted butter, vanilla essence and approx. 2 tbsp of water in another bowl and whisk well.
3. Add the flour mixture and chocolate chips and mix gently with help of a spatula to make a batter of dropping consistency.
4. Pour equal quantity of the batter into 6 greased and dusted 68 mm. (2½") diameter aluminum moulds.
5. Bake in a pre-heated oven at 200°C (400°F) for 10 minutes and at 150°C (300°F) for 15 to 20 minutes or till done. The sponge is done when it leaves the sides of the mould and is springy to touch.
6. Allow it to cool completely (approx. 30 minutes). Keep aside.

For the frosting
1. Put the butter in a deep bowl and beat it using a spatula.
2. Add the icing sugar and melted chocolate and mix well. Keep aside.

How to proceed
1. Fill the frosting in a piping bag as shown on page 20 and pipe out swirls of your choice on each cupcake.
2. Garnish each cupcake with chocolate chips and edible silver balls and serve immediately.

Choco Almond Cupcake

Chocolate and almond are a made-for-each other combination—and they present an unforgettable duet in this luxurious cupcake. Almond, almond essence and melted chocolate make the frosting very different from the rest of the cupcakes; and a cherry on top gives the perfect finish to it! Make it an unforgettable after-dinner treat, by serving with chocolate ice-cream, topped with almonds.

Preparation Time: 5 minutes. **Cooking Time: Nil.** **Makes 6 cupcakes.**

6 chocolate sponge, page 58

For the frosting
6 tbsp butter (at room temperature)
12 tbsp icing sugar
4½ tbsp melted chocolate mixed with 1 tsp milk
3 tbsp powdered almonds
½ tsp almond essence

For the garnish
6 tbsp soaked, deskinned and chopped almonds
6 cherries

For the frosting
1. Put the butter in a bowl and beat it using a spatula.
2. Add the icing sugar and mix well.
3. Add the melted chocolate, powdered almonds and almond essence, mix well and keep aside.

How to proceed
1. Fill the frosting in a piping bag as shown on page 20 and pipe out swirls of your choice on each cupcake.
2. Garnish each cupcake with almonds covering the frosting evenly, top with a cherry and serve immediately.

Coffee Walnut Cupcake

The bitterness of coffee and the nuttiness of walnut combine well to qualify this fabulous dessert as a great choice for connoisseurs. Walnuts add the required crunch to these cupcakes, while the coffee decoction imparts a very mature flavour. Follow the exact procedure mentioned here for making the coffee decoction, in order to ensure the best flavour. Garnish with silver balls for a perfect finishing touch.

Preparation Time: 5 minutes. Cooking Time: Nil. Makes 6 cupcakes.
Baking Temperature and Time: 200°C (400°F) for 15 minutes. 150°C (300°F) for 15 to 20 minutes.

For the vanilla coffee walnut sponge
¾ cup plain flour (*maida*)
¾ tsp baking powder
¼ tsp soda bi-carbonate
½ cup (200 gms) condensed milk
3 tbsp melted butter
½ tsp vanilla essence
3 tbsp chopped walnuts (*akhrot*)
2 tsp coffee powder dissolved in 4 tsp of hot water

For the frosting
6 tbsp butter (at room temperature)
12 tbsp icing sugar
1½ tsp coffee powder dissolved in 1 tbsp of hot water

For the garnish
Edible silver balls

For the vanilla coffee walnut sponge
1. Sieve the plain flour, baking powder and soda bi-carb together in a bowl and keep aside.
2. Combine the condensed milk, melted butter, vanilla essence and approx. 2 tbsp of water in another bowl and whisk well.
3. Add the flour mixture, walnuts and coffee mixture and mix gently with help of a spatula to make a batter of dropping consistency.
4. Pour equal quantity of the batter into 6 greased and dusted 68 mm. (2½") diameter aluminum moulds.
5. Bake in a pre-heated oven at 200°C (400°F) for 10 minutes and at 150°C (300°F) for 15 to 20 minutes or till done. The sponge is done when it leaves the sides of the mould and is springy to touch.
6. Allow it to cool completely (approx. 30 minutes). Keep aside.

For the frosting
1. Put the butter in a bowl and beat it using a spatula.
2. Add the icing sugar and mix well.
3. Add the coffee mixture, mix well and keep aside.

How to proceed
1. Fill the frosting in a piping bag as shown on page 20 and pipe out small swirls of your choice on each cupcake.
2. Garnish each cupcake with edible silver balls and serve immediately.

Tarla Dalal's

Dessert Collection

Mithai

Ice-creams & Frozen Desserts

The Chocolate Cook Book

Eggless Desserts

Desserts Under 10 Minutes

Microwave Snacks and Desserts

Cakes & Pastries

Low Calorie Sweets